Dupie

The life and times of a college
student as seen through the pen of
Campus Cartoonist
Gil Morales

Published by
The Dupie Press
Stanford, California

Dupie

Published by The Dupie Press, Stanford, California
Printed in the United States of America
Copyright 1981 by Gil Morales and Brett Kingstone — The Dupie Press. All rights reserved under international and Pan-American Copyright Conventions, including the right to reproduce this book or portions thereof, in any form. All inquiries should be addressed to:

    The Dupie Press
    P.O. Box 5771
    Stanford, California 94305

Back Cover Photo: John Sudick
Inside Cover Photo: Bob Deyling
Typesetting: ASSU Typesetting, Stanford, California.

Manufactured in the United States of America

A special thanks to Ann Reynolds and Bob Beyers of the
        Stanford News and Publications Office

Library of Congress
Catalog Number 81-68823

International Standard Book Number 0-940996-00-6

To Phoenix and Mother Alpha.

Foreword

I like to get up early. I mean *early*. Like 5:30. In the morning.

Why, you may ask, would any self-respecting college dean (of anything) roll out of the sack at *that* hour?

Well, partly because that's when the campus is at its prettiest. Partly because I get more work done between six and eight than between eight and six. (Committees, fortunately, *never* meet before nine in the morning.)

And partly because, thanks to the early delivery schedule of *The Stanford Daily*, I get to read "Dupie" with breakfast.

Like everyone else, I have habits. Needing a daily dose of humor is one of them. Long before Norman Cousins had discovered the curative powers of laughter, I had amassed a medicine chest full of tonics and elixirs: George Booth, Edward Koren, George Price, Charles Adams, William Hamilton, Bill Mauldin, Charles Schulz, Jeff MacNelly, and Gil Morales.

The arrangement is mutual. They contribute to my health, And, by buying their books, I undoubtedly contribute to theirs. But I've only *met* one of them: Gil Morales. *His* good health is in *your* hands.

Gil came into my life a little over four years ago. He was just your average excellent incoming freshman. Or, rather, mine. I did not suspect then what I suspect now. That he has a pet genie. I don't know where he keeps it, or what its sex is, or whether he's breaking any rules with it.

As you will see, Dupie takes a lot of walks. He apparently runs into all kinds of creatures popping up out of the grass. Or he runs into kamikaze flies and flowers that play dead in order to get fed. His is a world where birds drop real bombs. If it's Gil, and not his genie, who lives in this anthropomorphic world, then I'm in trouble. Stanford's in trouble. We've just given this guy a degree in Economics!

But Dupie's not all birds and bees (though he does raise the nettlesome question of the false expectations raised by always pairing these two in discussing sex). He's also the literate non-scientist who is alternately impressed and depressed by the world of science, even wondering out loud whether conceiving a baby in a test tube is *really* as much of a feat as conceiving one in the back seat of a '57 VW.

He's also some part of some part of all of us as we wend, or wended, our way through college. He's the student who found the only restful recovery from a three-day weekend was attending class.

Was your reasoning in determining when to study *really* more rational than that of picking petals off a daisy ("I will study, I will not study. . . .")? And didn't you wonder, along with the rest of us, whether "infinity" was just a term for the number of ways in which the food service could camouflage the meatloaf?

Dupie isn't all college students, or even all of one college student. A professor of English at Stanford once wisely remarked that part of what one ought to get from a good education is the "quality of your idle moments, your play." Dupie is the mind of one college student "at play."

Whether he is Gil's genie, or simply his imagination, Dupie is a healthy reminder to all of us of the potency of humor for putting things in perspective.

Be it the trauma associated with being *admitted* to college (do we really use a spinner or a ouija board, as everyone suspects?), or the trauma associated with actually *graduating* ("exit anxiety," as the counseling service calls it), Dupie has his fun with it.

While I don't understand the world as the economists see it, I do understand the world as Dupie sees it. Enough said.

Fred Hargadon
Dean of Admissions

July 1981
Stanford University

A Small Dupie Scrapbook:

Stanford Band Handbook

1979-80

Cover for the notorious Leland Stanford Junior University Marching Band's general guide to drugs, sex, and violence.
June '79

Poster for a concert performance by Stanford's renowned all-male choral and instrumental musical group. March 1980

THE **MENDICANTS** SPRING CONCERT

THURSDAY MAY 22ND 8:30 P.M. MEMORIAL CHURCH ADMISSION FREE

Welcome to the Farm

JUST WHAT have you gotten yourself into? After considering all your options, you've made your decision. You've put all your marbles in one basket; you're bound for Stanford in the fall.

What you will find when you get here defies generalization. Stanford will offer you an extraordinary number of opportunities; the directions you take will be your own. *Approaching Stanford* has been designed to introduce you to the Stanford community, calm your fears, and answer your questions. We haven't tried to answer them all; the discovery of Stanford is largely an individual journey.

One thing you needn't worry about is your ability to succeed here. There are no admissions mistakes. You have as much to offer Stanford as Stanford has to offer you. New friends, new outlooks, and new adventures all await you. Read on with curiosity and enthusiasm and realize that your approach to Stanford will soon culminate in the excitement of being here. Welcome! We're anxious to meet you.

If you're constantly questioning yourself, you had better be looking for the answers as well.

It took me until my senior year to realize that I wanted to be a freshman all my life.

My roommate and I have a strange and unique relationship: he's strange and I'm unique.

A page from *Approaching Stanford*, a publication for incoming freshmen, which is filled with several of my illustrations.
April 1981

The Stanford AlumniAlmanac

Published by the Stanford Alumni Association   Senior Edition/June 1981

This publication came out at graduation, and contained a listing of graduating seniors' addresses and future plans.

Cover for a new student magazine which started up in 1980. Having lost money on previous issues, the editors and founders put out this issue as a last-ditch attempt to recoup their losses, and so came to me for a cover. I also contributed a number of cartoons to the guts of the magazine. The issue, as it turned out, did fairly well, selling out in five days.

© 1978 By Gil Morales, Stanford, Ca.

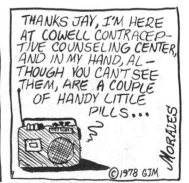

IN OTHER NEWS, THE DEPARTMENT OF ATHLETICS HAS REPORTED ITS OWN DEVELOPMENT, ALONG WITH THE PENTAGON, OF A NEW GENERATION OF NUCLEAR WEAPONRY...

...WHICH IS EXPECTED TO BE USED AS A BARGAINING TOOL IN THE FORTHCOMING SALT TALKS.

ACCORDING TO SOURCES HIGH IN THE DEPARTMENT, THE NEW WEAPON WAS DEVELOPED BY...

16-15

...INSTALLING A NUCLEAR WARHEAD IN DARRIN NELSON'S FOOTBALL HELMET

©1978 GJM

I WAS WONDERING, IAN, WHY DOES UC BERKELEY CALL ITSELF 'CAL' AND NOT 'BERKELEY'?

BECAUSE 'BERKELY' SOUNDS LIKE SOMEONE WHO'S THROWING UP A DINNER CONSISTING OF MASSIVE AMOUNTS OF VEAL PARMEJAN.

BERKELEY BERKELEY BERRRRRKELY!

16-16

WILDLY.

©1978 GJM

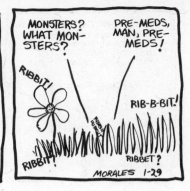

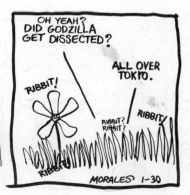

HAVE YOU EVER NOTICED HOW THE BIRDS AROUND HERE ARE SO TAME?

HMMPH... DON'T LET 'EM FOOL YOU...

THEY'RE ACTUALLY CIA AGENTS.

SO YOU THINK THE BIRDS AROUND HERE ARE ACTUALLY CIA AGENTS?

UH-HUH...

WELL, IF THEY'RE CIA AGENTS, HOW DO THEY ALL GET TO BE SO SHORT?

THEY'RE SPECIALLY BRED.

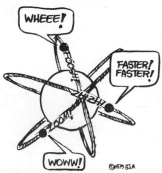

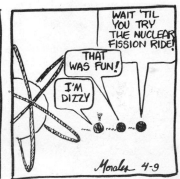

SAY, WOULD YOU LIKE TO GO TO THE BEACH THIS AFTERNOON?

ONLY IF WE GO TO A BEACH WHERE THERE'S LOTS OF GUYS IN SPEEDO SWIMMING TRUNKS...

WHAT FOR!?

©1979 GJM

...GOOD VISUALS.

SEXIST...

Morales 4-23

WELL, HERE I AM, ABOUT TO ENTER MY FIRST FRATERNITY RUSH PARTY...I WONDER IF THIS IS THE RIGHT HOUSE...

...HEY, THERE'S SOMEONE LOOKING OUT THE SECOND STORY WINDOW. I THINK I'LL ASK HIM...

TINKLE TINKLE

©1979 GJM

TINKLE TINKLE

WELL, ON SECOND THOUGHT, HE LOOKS A LITTLE BUSY...

Morales 4-24

THE EARLY BIRD GETS THE WORM...

© 1979 GJM

THE REST GO TO McDONALD'S...

Morales 5-3

GAWDAMMIT! I JUST WAITED TWO HOURS IN LINE AND I STILL COULDN'T GET ANY G★⊘#! GAS!

WELL, TODAY I ONLY WAITED IN LINE FOR 5 MINUTES AND I GOT PLENTY OF GAS...

OH YEAH? WHERE AT?

© 1979 GJM

DORMITORY FOOD SERVICE...

Morales 5-11

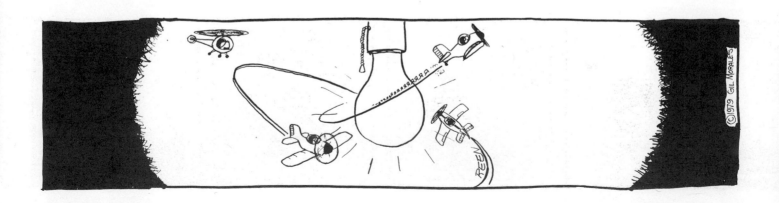

...SO ANYWAY, IAN, I DO HAVE A JOB FOR THE SUMMER... OH, AND MY DAD IS STILL HASSLING ME ABOUT MY MAJOR...

HE SAYS I SHOULD GET A DEGREE IN A FIELD THAT WILL BE USEFUL AND RELEVANT AFTER I FINISH SCHOOL

OF COURSE, I HAD TO EXPLAIN TO HIM...

...THAT STANFORD DOESN'T OFFER A DEGREE IN UNEMPLOYMENT.

© 1979 GIL MORALES

TODAY ON OUR SHOW WE HAVE WITH US MRS. OMAR BRANDLE, WHO AT THE AGE OF 124 IS THE WORLD'S OLDEST LIVING HUMAN BEING. TELL US, MRS. BRANDLE, TO WHAT DO YOU OWE YOUR LONG LIFE?

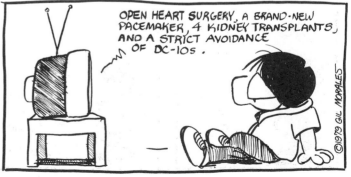

OPEN HEART SURGERY, A BRAND-NEW PACEMAKER, 4 KIDNEY TRANSPLANTS, AND A STRICT AVOIDANCE OF DC-10s.

© 1979 GIL MORALES

MADIGAN, SON, I WANT YOU TO KNOW THAT RIGHT NOW YOUR MOTHER IS UPSTAIRS CRYING...

...BECAUSE SHE WAS LOOKING THROUGH YOUR DRESSER AND FOUND THIS BAG OF MARIJUANA.

NEEDLESS TO SAY, SHE'S VERY DISAPPOINTED...

...SHE WAS HOPING TO FIND SOME VALIUM...

TELL HER I'LL CHECK WITH MY DEALER FIRST THING IN THE MORNING

©1979 GIL MORALES

MADIGAN, SON, CAN I SPEAK WITH YOU FOR A MINUTE?

YEAH, DAD. WHADDAYA NEED?

I JUST WANT TO TELL YOU, SON, THAT IF YOU'RE GOING TO STAY HOME THIS SUMMER I'LL HAVE TO ASK THAT YOU BE A BIT MORE DISCRETE WITH YOUR DRUG USE...

YOU MEAN...

THAT'S RIGHT, NO MORE HALLUCINOGENS AT THE DINNER TABLE.

AW, DAD!

©1979 Gil Morales

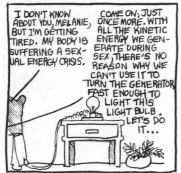

I DON'T KNOW ABOUT YOU, MELANIE, BUT I'M GETTING TIRED. MY BODY IS SUFFERING A SEXUAL ENERGY CRISIS.

COME ON, JUST ONCE MORE. WITH ALL THE KINETIC ENERGY WE GENERATE DURING SEX, THERE'S NO REASON WHY WE CAN'T USE IT TO TURN THE GENERATOR FAST ENOUGH TO LIGHT THIS LIGHT BULB. LET'S DO IT...

PANT, PANT, PANT, PANT, PANT, PANT...

BING!

SQUEAK SQUEAK SQUEAK SQUEAK

HEY! IT'S WORKING!

IT IS! WE'VE FINALLY PROVED THAT SEX CAN BE USED AS AN ALTERNATIVE ENERGY SOURCE. DO YOU REALIZE WHAT THIS MEANS?

YEAH, THAT SEX IS GOING TO BE REGULATED BY THE DEPARTMENT OF ENERGY.

WELL, THAT'S THE PRICE WE PAY FOR PROGRESS.

Gil Morales — 10-11

GOOD EVENING. IN TODAY'S NEWS, CIA OFFICIALS HAVE RELEASED INFRA-RED PHOTOGRAPHS REVEALING THE PRESENCE OF AT LEAST TWO SOVIET SAILORS IN A ROWBOAT 250 MILES OFF SHORE OF CALIFORNIA.

ACCORDING TO ONE CIA OFFICIAL, SUCH AN UNPRECEDENTED BUILD-UP OF SOVIET NAVAL PERSONNEL OFF THE SHORE OF CALIFORNIA POSES A SERIOUS THREAT TO THE SECURITY OF THE UNITED STATES...

HOWEVER, PRESIDENT CARTER HAS ELECTED TO SEEK A DIPLOMATIC SOLUTION TO THE CRISIS, DESPITE CRIES FROM THE PENTAGON CALLING FOR A SWIFT AND EXPEDIENT TORPEDO STRIKE ON THE PART OF THE NAVY.

© 1979 GJM

FILM AT ELEVEN.

Gil Morales — 10-17

GIL MORALES 11-20

RING! RING!

HELLO?... NO, MADIGAN ISN'T IN AT THE MOMENT.

WELL, THE LAST TIME I SAW HIM HE HAD JUST FINISHED DRINKING A 32 OZ. MARTINI, STARTED TO MUMBLE SOMETHING ABOUT NERD-HUNTING SEASON OPENING TODAY, AND THEN HEADED FOR THE LIBRARY.

ALRIGHT, DROP YOUR CALCULATOR AND COME ALONG QUIETLY...

?

©1980 Gil Whitnel 2-6

YOU KNOW, I'VE NEVER PLAYED BASKETBALL BEFORE...

DON'T WORRY YOU'LL LEARN. HERE, I'LL LET YOU HAVE THE BALL FIRST.

ALRIGHT, WHAT DO I DO NOW?

SHOOT THE BALL...

OH, OKAY!

BLAM!

DO I WIN?

©1980 Gil Whitnel 2-8

AND NOW TO TEST THE FORMULA WHICH WILL ENABLE ME TO PASS 35 UNITS WORTH OF CLASSES THIS SPRING DESPITE THE NUMEROUS TEMPTATIOUS DISTRACTIONS...

BOTTOMS UP!

GLUG GLUG
GLUG GLUG
GLUG GLUG

...BY CHANGING ME... ARRGH!...FROM MY PRESENT SELF... UGGHH! AAR! ERRGH!...INTO, INTO...

CRASH!

SPLASH!

MR. NERD...

© 1980 Gil Morales 4-1

GOOD EVENING, FELLOW UNDERDOG LOVERS. IT IS WITH GREAT PLEASURE THAT I INTRODUCE OUR GUEST SPEAKER FOR TONIGHT'S MEETING OF "STANFORD STUDENTS FOR ANDERSON."

JUST BECAUSE JOHN ANDERSON IS INTELLIGENT, STRAIGHT-FORWARD, NOT WELL KNOWN, AND NOT A FORMER B-MOVIE ACTOR DOESN'T MEAN HE CAN'T BE ELECTED PRESIDENT!

SO, WITHOUT FURTHER ADO, HERE HE IS, THE UNKNOWN CANDIDATE HIMSELF, JOHN ANDERSON!

HI THERE. HAVE YOU HEARD THE ONE ABOUT RONALD REAGAN O.D.-ING ON GERITOL...

CLAP
CLAP
CLAP
CLAP
CLAP

© 1980 Gil Morales 4-3

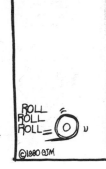

MADIGAN, WILL YOU CALM DOWN!?!

NO! I'VE GOT TO STOP HIM BEFORE IT'S TOO LATE!

STOP! DON'T DO IT! DON'T DO IT!

@#★☺!

COME ON MADIGAN! THIS IS A FREE COUNTRY!

WAIT! STOP! DON'T DO IT! YOU'LL REGRET IT LATER!

IF THE GUY WANTS TO VOTE FOR RONALD REAGAN THERE'S NOTHING YOU CAN DO ABOUT IT!

YOU FOOL! STOP! THINK ABOUT WHAT YOU'RE DOING!

©1980 Gil Morales 11-4

HEE HEE, HERE COMES DUPIE IN HIS DINO THE DINOSAUR INFLATABLE RUBBER LIFE PRESERVER. I THINK I'LL FLIP HIM A FEW DEROGATORY WITTICISMS.

WAIT A MINUTE... HE SEEMS TO BE APPROACHING AWFULLY FAST...

UH-OH... I THINK THIS POOL IS ABOUT TO BECOME UNSAFE FOR A CERTAIN SWIMMER IN THIS VICINITY.

©1980 Gil Morales 10-5

RAMMING SPEED!

RRRRR RRRRR RRRRR

YOU CAN'T BACK OUT NOW, MADIGAN. I'VE ALREADY MADE ARRANGEMENTS WITH YOUR DATE

NO WAY.

I'M LOSING MY PATIENCE.

DON'T WORRY, YOU'LL FIND IT AGAIN.

NOW COME ON, YOU HAVE TO GO!

YOU'LL HAVE TO DRAG ME AWAY.

FORTUNATELY, I HAD ENOUGH SENSE NOT TO SAY, "OVER MY DEAD BODY."

SPAGHETTI, YES.
WORMS, NO.

HERE IT IS, THE END OF
THE QUARTER, AND I'M
STUCK IN THE LIBRARY AT
10:30 ON A SATURDAY
NIGHT WITH NO END
IN SIGHT

WHAT COULD
BE LONELIER?

AH ALWAYS CARRIES A TIN OF SHMOAL CHEWIN' TOBAKKER WIT...

CUT! CUT!!

WHAT'S WRONG? IS IT MY DELIVERY? MY MAKE-UP?

NO, IT'S YOUR SPURS. THEY'RE DIFFERENT

WHAT'S WRONG WITH MINIATURE REPLICAS OF MERCEDES BENZ SPOKE-RIMMED WHEELS?

EVERYTHING. CHANGE 'EM.

HA! AND YOU CALL THIS HOLLYWOOD!

1-8

©1980 Gil Morales

ALRIGHT, LET'S TAKE IT FROM THE MID-WAY POINT...ER AND FEEL FREE TO AD LIB...IT ADDS CHARACTER...ROLL 'EM!

SHMOAL CHEWIN' TOBAKKER GIVES ME REEL TOBAKKER TASTE WIDDOUT LATIN UP... JES' A WAD BETWEEN YER CHEEK END GUM...

...AIND YOU KEN GROSS OUT ALLA YER FRIENDS BY SPITTIN' OUT A PYOOTRID, DARK-GREENISH YELLER GLOB A' SALIVA AND TOBAKKER

LAK THIS.

PTEW

SPLAT!

CUT! CUT!!

©1980 Gil Morales 1-9

YOU KNOW, I'VE BEEN WATCHING YOU FOR A WHOLE HOUR, AND ALL I'VE SEEN YOU DO IS STARE AT THAT BOOK.

THAT'S RIGHT. IT'S CALLED PROCRASTI-NATION. YOU'LL LEARN ABOUT IT WHEN YOU'RE OLDER...

OH, I GET IT, IT'S LIKE INEB-RIATION... MOM SAID I'D LEARN ABOUT THAT WHEN I GOT OLDER TOO

THAT'S RIGHT, A FEW MORE YEARS AND YOU'LL KNOW ALL ABOUT ALL THOSE VICES...

BUT FIRST YOU'LL NEED SOME TIME TO DEVELOP YOUR SHORTCOMINGS

©1981 Gil Morales 1-28

GULP! HEY DUPIE! DO YOU HAVE A STOP WATCH?

A STOPWATCH? WHAT DO YOU NEED A STOP WATCH FOR? FINISH YOUR MILK AND COOK IES AND GO TO BED...

SQUILCH!

I NEED IT FOR DIPPING MY COOK-IES IN MILK... IF I DON'T DIP THEM FOR EXACTLY 2.7 SECONDS THEY DON'T COME OUT RIGHT. THEY'LL BE TOO DRY OR TOO SOGGY!

WHAT!?

AND IF THEY'RE TOO SOGGY THEY FALL TO THE BOTTOM AND LOOK REALLY GROSS AND THEN YOU CAN'T DRINK THE MILK SO YOU HIDE IT IN THE CLOSET SO MOM WON'T YELL AT YOU FOR WASTING IT AND IT TURNS INTO A MOLD CULTURE.

SORRY, I DON'T HAVE A STOP WATCH.

IN THAT CASE, COULD I EX-CHANGE MY MILK AND COOK-IES FOR KAHLUA AND MILK?

GO TO BED.

©1981 Gil Morales 1-29

DID YOU KNOW THAT REAGAN'S SECRETARY OF THE INTERIOR IS IN FAVOR OF LETTING OIL COMPANIES DRILL OFF THE CALIFORNIA COAST?

WHAT!? AND RUIN THE SURFING!? BOY, THAT BURNS ME UP!

KA-CHUNG KA-CHUNG KA-CHUNG KA-CHUNG KA-CHU

THOSE MERCENARY OLD CORPORATE GEEZERS DON'T CARE IF THEY RUIN THE ENVIRONMENT, THEY JUST WANT TO PAD THEIR PENSION FUNDS SO THEY CAN LIVE IT UP BEFORE THEY KICK OFF AND LEAVE ALL THE PROBLEMS THEY CREATED TO US...

KACHUNG KACHUNG KACHUNG

THAT'S OKAY, THOUGH... INSTANT KARMA WILL GET THEM.

WHAT DO YOU MEAN?

THEY'RE ALL GOING TO BE REINCARNATED AS CATALYTIC CONVERTERS...

©1981 Gil Morales 2-19

HEY, DUPIE, WHY SO BLUE?

LOOK AT ALL THIS WORK I HAVE TO DO... TERM PAPERS, TOMES TO READ, PROBLEM SETS FROM HERE TO ETERNITY...

WHAT YOU NEED, MY FINE FRIEND, ARE EXTREME POWERS OF RATIONALIZATION... HERE, LET ME PUT ALL OF THIS ACADEMIC NONSENSE INTO MY HAT...

NOW FOR THE MAGIC WORDS: "WE HAVE ARRIVED AT THAT JUNCTION, WHEREUPON OUR BRAINS FUNCTION LIKE TAR AND MOLASSES, SO LET'S BLOW OFF CLASSES THE WEATHER DECREES BY INJUNCTION, AND... PRESTO!

TAP TAP TAP

YOUR STUDIES HAVE BEEN TRANSFORMED INTO A HARMLESS, DOCILE, LITTLE BUNNY RABBIT...

MY TA'S ARE GONNA LOVE THIS...

©1981 Gil Morales 2-23

DUPIE! ARE YOU HOME?

HE'S IN THE BACK FEEDING THE BIRDS...

OH.

HE'S REALLY INTO IT...

I'VE NOTICED.

GET EXCITED PALS, THIS PROMISES TO BE BEAK-SMACK-ING DELICIOUS.

HEY MADIGAN! LOOK AT THIS!

HOLY COW! WHAT IS THAT?!

I'M NOT SURE...

IT MUST BE AN UNIDENTIFIED FLYING OBJECT...

ACTUALLY, I'M JUST FLYING INCOGNITO.

OOF

HOW DO YOU LIKE MY PRESENT FROM THE EASTER BUNNY?

WOW! IS IT FILLED WITH CHOCOLATE? LET'S CONSUME IT IMMEDIATELY!

WELL, IT ISN'T CHOCOLATE, BUT WE CAN CONSUME ITS CONTENTS IMMEDIATELY IF YOU LIKE

PLOP!

YOU GO GET SOME ICE AND A TUB, AND I'LL PUT THE TAP IN...

SOME PEOPLE ADVOCATE LEGISLATING GUN CONTROL

TWIRL
TWIRL

FLIP

OOPS.

BLAM!

PERSONALLY, I JUST NEED MORE PRACTICE ON MINE.

4.20

© 1981 Gil Morales 5-7

© 1981 Gil Morales 5-8

HIC, HICCUP! ... BURP! OHHHHHHHHHHHHHHHHH...

OH WOW.... HICCUP! WHO WON THE WAR?

WAIT, WAIT, NOW I REMEMBER! IT WAS BEER! A WHOLE CASE OF IT! BILLIONS UPON BILLIONS OF ETHANOL MOLECULES WREAKING HAVOC ON MY BRAIN. MY FINITE SUPPLY OF BRAIN CELLS HAS BECOME EVEN MORE FINITE... HIC!

©1979 GVH

BUT WHAT THE HELL, I GO TO COLLEGE, I'VE GOT PLENTY OF EXTRA BRAIN CELLS.

©1981 Gil Morales 10-5

CRACK!

CRACK!

©1981 Gil Morales 5-18

RADIOACTIVE CHICKEN EGGS ARE A GREAT WAY TO ENTERTAIN YOUR FRIENDS...

YOU KNOW, I'LL NEVER UNDERSTAND WHY HUMANS ALWAYS TALK ABOUT THE "BIRDS AND THE BEES" WHEN EXPLAINING SEX TO THEIR OFFSPRING.

I CAN UNDERSTAND TALKING ABOUT BIRDS AND BIRDS, OR EVEN BEES AND BEES...

BUT BIRDS AND BEES? WHY, THAT'S DOWNRIGHT KINKY!

GO TELL THAT TO MY PARENTS, PAL.

©1981 Gil Morales 5-19

EGADS! WHAT IS THIS WEIRD STUFF WE'RE HAVING FOR DINNER!?

IT'S SEA SQUID

WIGGLE WIGGLE

THIS IS TOTALLY WEIRD.

NO IT'S NOT, IT'S A 'DELICACY.'

WIGGLE WIGGLE WIGGLE

OH YEAH!? WELL WHAT DOES THAT MEAN?

WIGGLE WIGGLE

IT'S TOTALLY WEIRD...

©1981 Gil Morales

NORMALLY, IN THE LOWER AIR SPACES IN WHICH I AM USED TO FLYING, THE LAWS OF NATURE PREVAIL...

BZZZ

YOU KNOW, SURVIVAL OF THE FITTEST, ETC., ETC...

ZOOM!

BZZZ

WHAP!

BUT SOMETIMES YOU JUST NEED A BIGGER MOUTH...

UH-OH, IT LOOKS LIKE WE'VE GOT A HEAVY SEA TODAY!

FORTUNATELY, I REMEMBERED TO BRING ALONG A BOTTLE OF VALIUM TABLETS!

I HOPE THIS IS ENOUGH!

TOSS

THOSE LITTLE PILLS ARE GREAT AT CALMING A ROUGH SEA...

©1981 Bil Alexander 5-29

About the Publishers

Brett Kingstone and Gil Morales are both 1981 graduates of Stanford University with degrees in economics. Brett, whose origins trace back to Long Beach, New York, is the publisher, financier, agent, and business manager for The Dupie Press. He is the author of a recently published book, *The Student Entrepreneur's Guide — How To Start and Run Your Own Part-Time Small Business* (Ten Speed Press, Berkeley, California, 1981), and devotes much of his time to running his own small business ventures, The Dupie Press included. Gil emerged from obscurity in Whittier, California to become the President, creator, author, and artist for the Dupie Press. His cartoon strips have appeared in the *Stanford Daily* throughout his college career, and he has contributed graphics to a number of Stanford campus publications.

Brett and Gil originally met when Brett sought Gil as a potential illustrator for his book, *The Student Entrepreneur's Guide*. Thus began a fruitful relationship which has resulted in the publication of this work and the concomitant creation of The Dupie Press. The two now share a house in Barron Park, California, as well as a fondness for motorcycles, guitars and women.

Dupie makes a great gift. To order more books, fill out the order form below and mail it along with a check or money order for $4.95 per copy (postage included) to:

The Dupie Press
P.O. Box 5771
Stanford, California 94305

Inquiries concerning the purchase of original cartoon strips (got any favorites?) hand-drawn by the author may be made on this same order form.

- -

Name _____

Address _____

City _____ State _____ Zip _____